MW01037725

WORDS *of* HOPE *and* HEALING

Understanding Your Grief
after a
DRUG-
OVERDOSE
DEATH

Companion Press is an imprint of the Center for Loss and Life Transition, 3735 Broken Bow Road, Fort Collins, Colorado 80526.

25   24   25   22   21   20   6   5   4   3   2   1

ISBN: 978-1-61722-285-6

WORDS *of* HOPE *and* HEALING

Understanding Your Grief
after a
DRUG-
OVERDOSE
DEATH

Alan D. Wolfelt, Ph.D.

Companion
PRESS

An imprint of the Center for Loss and Life Transition | Fort Collins, Colorado

CONTENTS

WELCOME

"Anything that's human is mentionable, and anything that is mentionable can be more manageable. When we talk about our feelings, they become less overwhelming, less upsetting, and less scary. The people we trust with that important talk can help us know that we are not alone."

— Fred Rogers

Loss is always hard, but when someone you love dies of an accidental drug overdose, the grief that follows can be especially painful and challenging.

I am sorry that you are faced with suffering such a difficult grief. I hope the words in this book will be a source of comfort and affirmation for you as you move through the early days of your grief and into the weeks and months to come.

First, it's essential for you to know that all of the thoughts, feelings, and behaviors you are experiencing right now are normal. Grief is what we feel inside whenever we lose someone we love. In addition to those normal and necessary feelings, your grief has been made more complex by the cause of the death and possibly the events in the life of your loved

1

one leading up to the death. Yet even though this grief may be more complicated than other griefs you have experienced in your life, it is still normal.

Second, please hold onto the belief that you can and will get through this. I have been a grief counselor and educator for more than forty years, and I have companioned a number of people whose loved ones died of drug overdose. They have asked me to share with you the message that not only can you survive what may right now seem unsurvivable, you can go on to find meaning and joy in life again. The principles in this book will help you step through the shadow of the valley of death and back into the light. No, your life will never be the same, but it can be good again.

And third, even in your darkest days, I want you to remember to foster hope. Hope is an expectation of a good that is yet to be. Hope is looking ahead and maintaining the awareness that there are good things coming. You will experience fun and joy again. There will come a day when the death is not the first or even the main thing you think about each day. So even as you are grieving, be on the lookout for ways to build hope into your life.

Thank you for entrusting me with companioning you on this path you did not choose. You are grieving the tragic death of someone you care about. And you will find your way back to hope and healing.

THE EARLY DAYS

"We don't heal in isolation, but in community."
— S. Kelley Harrell

As someone grieving an overdose death, you deserve special understanding and care.

In fact, especially in the early days after the death, I want you to think of yourself as in need of intensive care. Remember that you have sustained a terrible emotional and spiritual injury. Just as if your body was badly wounded, your heart and soul need intensive TLC right now.

During these early days, allow others to take care of you. Accept their gifts of food and attention. When they ask what they can do for you, suggest something. If it feels comforting, ask others to simply be present to you. Having people nearby to make you a sandwich, to talk with you, to help you make funeral and other arrangements, and even just to sit in sacred silence with you can help you feel safe and supported as you move through the blur of the first hours, days, and weeks after the death.

And give yourself as much resting time as possible. Take time off work if at all possible. Let household and other nonessential chores wait for right now. In the early weeks and months after the death, don't expect to—indeed, don't try to—carry on with your normal routine.

Feelings of shock and numbness are typical at first. Overdose deaths are often sudden and unexpected, which heightens the normal shock and numbness of grief. You may feel a sense of disbelief. You might feel like you're walking around in a daze. You may be moving through your days yet feel like you're not really there. This is normal.

Have you been imagining that the person who died might text you or walk through the door at any moment? Do you catch yourself looking for the person in passing cars or in crowds? These are also normal reactions, especially in cases of sudden and unexpected death.

In the early days, you might also struggle with questions about whether the death was preventable or not. You may find yourself obsessing about the person's circumstances on the day or week of the death. You might also be unsure if the death was intentional or not—and this can be an especially terrible uncertainty to come to terms with. It's normal, though painful, to think about such uncertainties.

Denial, too, is a natural companion to shock and numbness in the early days. You might find yourself pushing away the reality of what has happened. You might not feel like learning or talking about the details of the circumstances of the death. If your loved one had been struggling with addiction for a long time, you might have been through a number of overdose close calls before, which can heighten feelings of denial and unreality when a death eventually happens. You also might realize in your mind that the person has died without fully feeling the understanding with your heart.

Thank goodness for shock, numbness, and denial. They are nature's way of protecting us from sudden, terrible realities. They are the shock absorbers that will help you survive the early days. As they begin to wear off, you will be able to slowly understand and embrace the full reality over time, bit by bit, day by day.

If you are still experiencing strong feelings of shock, numbness, and denial, be sure to practice good self-care (see pg. 29) and reach out to others for support. And when you're ready, talking to good, nonjudgmental listeners about your thoughts and feelings is an effective way to begin to get unstuck if you're feeling stuck in shock, numbness, and denial.

THE FUNERAL FOR YOUR LOVED ONE

If the funeral for your loved one has not yet taken place, I encourage you to have a ceremony that honors the qualities you and your family loved best and will miss most about the person who died. The cause of the death cannot take away these precious characteristics and memories. Personalize the funeral as much as possible by incorporating music, readings, video/photo tributes, and remembrances that tell the unique story of the life of the person who died.

Funerals are so important to mourners because they help us meet our mourning needs (see pg. 19). Funerals may be *about* the person who died, but they are *for* the living. The funeral you plan and participate in for the person who died will not only give you a structure that will help hold you up during the first days of your grief, it will provide you with the life-affirming support of friends and family. Choosing not to have a funeral service, on the other hand, only creates a void where all that love and support would otherwise be.

During the funeral and in the obituary, consider being honest about the cause of death. The stigma surrounding overdose deaths (see pg. 9) is unfortunate and harmful. If we as a society and culture are to move past this stigma, we must have open dialogue about drug use and addiction. You may feel an impulse to keep the circumstances of this death private, but such secrecy will ultimately only hinder your healing as well as the healing of others who mourn the loss of the precious person who died.

At the same time, it's important to remember that the funeral is about so much more than the cause of death. Most of all, the funeral is about telling the story of the life and the love.

ADDICTION AND THE
OPIOID EPIDEMIC

"Opioids can lull people who use them into a false sense of security at first. But the drugs can quickly begin to rewire their brains, stripping them of other sources of pleasure and making it increasingly difficult to cope with the trials of everyday life while sober. By the time some people realize they are dependent, they may already be deep in the throes of addiction, a dark pit from which it is incredibly hard to climb out."

— Jennifer Harlan

While some people who die of accidental drug overdose are just beginning to experiment with drugs, or use occasionally, most overdose deaths are associated with escalating drug abuse and addiction. Concurrent alcohol abuse is also common.

As you may be all too aware, people of all ages, backgrounds, and socioeconomic levels are affected by addiction. Addiction is a recognized disease in which the pleasure centers of the brain get taken over by the need for the drug. Addicts cannot fully control their behavior, though many of them try and succeed for periods of time.

In the United States today, the majority of drug-overdose deaths involve an opioid, such as prescription painkillers, fentanyl, or heroin. More than ten million Americans misuse opioids each year, and well over 100 die every day from overdose. That's more people than die of traffic fatalities. In fact, opioid use and overdose trends have grown so devastating that the U.S. Department of Health & Human Services has labeled the problem an epidemic.

What all of this means is that you are not alone. Millions upon millions of families and friends have lost a loved one to drug use. This doesn't make the death of the unique person you cared about any less tragic, but it does mean that there are probably resources in your community specifically designed to help you. What's more, some of your friends and neighbors have likely lived through a similar experience. You need not walk alone. Befriending others who understand what it's like to have loved and lost someone precious to drugs is often one of the best ways to find your way back to hope and healing.

STIGMATIZED GRIEF AND THE FORGOTTEN MOURNER

"Maybe 'letting go with love' means letting go of the silence."
— Sandy Swenson

Even though addiction is a disease that can affect anyone, unfortunately there is still a social stigma associated with drug-overdose deaths. For you, a person who has lost someone special, this can seem doubly unfair. Not only has someone you cared about died, but others may avoid you or make you feel ashamed about the death.

Because of this stigma, you are at risk for becoming what I call a "forgotten mourner." You may have friends or family members who feel uncomfortable about the cause of death, so, because they don't know how to respond, fall out of touch with you. Others might assume you don't want to talk about or be reminded of the death, so they act as if it never happened. Still others harbor the irrational but still very real fear that if they talk about drug use and overdose, it could happen to their family, too.

The problem is that you do need the love and support of others, especially now. To be a forgotten mourner is to feel alone and unacknowledged. That is a lonely, terrible place to be.

There are a number of things you can do to break through this wall of isolation. Remind yourself that your friend or family member died of a common, deadly disease. Learn more about opioid use and how it's affecting so many people. Reach out to others impacted by overdose death.

Above all, talk openly about both the death and its effects on you and your family whenever you get the chance. Shining a light of openness and empathy on overdose deaths will help you and others heal. It will also make others feel more comfortable about reaching out to you and bringing up the death.

WHAT YOU MIGHT THINK AND FEEL

"One of the underreported manifestations of the opioid-overdose epidemic now sweeping the United States is the sheer volume of complicated grief experienced by the surviving loved ones of those who died of an overdose. Feelings of shame, stigma, guilt, anger, blame, shock, and isolation put a heavy burden on those impacted by an overdose death—including parents, spouses, siblings, children, grandparents, and friends—and they may not believe they have a safe place to talk about it."

— Larry Beresford, in *The Lancet*

In addition to **SHOCK, NUMBNESS, AND DENIAL**, you are likely to experience a wide range of thoughts and feelings as you grieve this death. First we'll talk about the most common feelings, then, in the section starting on page 19 entitled "Your Six Needs of Mourning," I'll suggest healthy ways to integrate and find relief from the feelings you find most difficult.

ANXIETY AND FEAR may arise, especially early on. You may feel blindsided by what happened. Your sense of safety and security in life has been threatened by this sudden, horrific event, so it's no wonder if you feel uneasy, anxious, or afraid. You may worry that something bad might happen to someone else you love, or to yourself. You might be anxious about finances or other practical matters. You might fear you are "going crazy" because of the powerful, disorganized thinking of your grief. You might even be afraid you can't survive this. In the aftermath of a drug overdose, in fact, many mourners report crippling anxiety. If this is true for you, please care for yourself by talking to your physician or a therapist about your anxiety.

SADNESS, of course, is part of any grief journey. It's normal—although so difficult—to be immersed in deep sorrow and pain. For most mourners, this is the hardest feeling to cope with. Many people who die of drug overdose are young, which compounds the hurt. Young people aren't supposed to die, and they're certainly not supposed to die before their parents and even grandparents. But regardless of the age of the person who died, you have every right to be sad. Someone precious in your life has been taken away from you. Allowing yourself to feel your sadness is in large part what your journey toward healing is all about.

Feelings of **GUILT AND REGRET** can sometimes go hand-in-hand with this sadness in cases of drug overdose. Parents of the person who died, grandparents, aunts and uncles, spouses or partners, teachers and other mentors—all may feel guilty for things they did or didn't do, said or didn't say. Overdose deaths often feel like they were avoidable. These "if-onlys" are normal and natural, even though what happened was not your fault or within your control.

SHAME is closely related to guilt and regret, but it is not the same. Guilt and regret are feelings you have about your own actions or inactions, while shame is something you experience when you believe that others are judging something intrinsic about you or your loved one. In other words, guilt is the feeling that you did something bad, while shame is the feeling, that you or your loved one *are* bad. When someone loved dies of drug overdose, shame is often part of the survivor experience because of the social stigma associated with drug use and addiction—which is something we as a culture need to work on changing. While if you have this feeling it will need, like all grief feelings, ongoing exploration and integration, please know that your loved one was not bad, and you are not bad—just human.

ANGER AND OTHER EXPLOSIVE EMOTIONS (such as hate, blame, resentment, and rage) after a drug-overdose death are also common and understandable. You may be angry at the person who died, for relapsing or for ignoring advice, good judgment, or safety protocols. You may be mad at others who helped get your loved one involved in drug use, supplied them with drugs, or enabled their dependence in any way. You might also be angry with God or a higher power over this terrible waste of human life. It might help you to understand that explosive emotions are essentially forms of protest. Understandably, you don't want to accept what has happened, and so you protest the reality. Like all other emotions in grief, protest emotions are normal.

In cases of overdose death, anger may come out as **BLAME.** This can be particularly hurtful. If you feel blamed for the death, or if you are blaming others, it's important to realize that what lies beneath blame are actually feelings of powerlessness and sadness. Yet mourners often feel justified in blaming others. Blame seems more powerful and action-oriented than hopelessness, guilt, and shame. And it often seems easier to live with anger and blame than the depths of despair. As with all explosive emotions, however, it's important to befriend and try to understand blame so you don't get stuck there.

Feelings of **RELIEF AND RELEASE** might also be a part of your grief journey. When someone dies who has been addicted to drugs for a long time and/or has had numerous relapses or close calls with death over the years, mourners sometimes feel as if they can finally breathe again. It's as if they have been holding their breath this entire time, worrying that the addicted person might die or harm someone else, and now that worry is finally over. The sequel to relief may be guilt. Survivors often feel guilty about feeling relieved, but this dimension of grief is also natural and does not equate to a lack of love for the person who died.

Of course, grief affects not only your heart but also your body, mind, and spirit.

Grief is **PHYSICALLY** demanding, especially after a sudden, traumatic death. The stress may make you more susceptible to illness and bodily discomfort. You may also feel lethargic, weak, or exceptionally fatigued. You may not be sleeping well, and you may have no appetite. Your stomach might hurt. Your chest may ache.

COGNITIVELY, it's common for mourners to report trouble concentrating, focusing, and completing simple tasks. Temporarily, you might also have a hard time with short-term memory.

SPIRITUALLY, you may be struggling with questions of faith, the meaning of life, or the possibility of an afterlife. You may be searching for reasons to get out of bed in the morning or go on living. Feelings of despair and purposelessness in grief are common and can be very hard to cope with.

Basically, **YOUR GRIEF MAY AFFECT EVERY ASPECT OF YOUR LIFE.** Nothing may feel "normal" for quite some time, and each day might be difficult. You might experience many different feelings all at once, and those feelings may change from day to day, or even from minute to minute.

If much of this is true for you, don't be alarmed. You aren't going crazy—you're grieving, and grieving a difficult death at that. Trust that in time and with the work of mourning we'll review next, you will eventually find your way to peace and a new normal. And in the meantime, even in the midst of your most challenging grief, you can also plan for and experience regular interludes of respite and relief.

OVERDOSE GRIEF AND YOUR FAMILY

Your family has suffered a traumatic death. Though the loss has affected the family as a whole, each person in your family will have different thoughts and feelings as they move through their grief.

It's normal for family relationships to be stressed. To counteract this stress, try to be accepting of each other's unique grief and mourning styles. Allow room for different understandings, interpretations, and expressions. Reserve judgment whenever possible. Extend love and compassion as much as possible.

And when the pressure cooker of shared but unique grief begins to boil over, reach out to helpers outside your family for support. Understandably, the stress of traumatic grief often prevents grieving family members from fully supporting each other. Within each grieving individual, there's a naturally high need for support and a low capacity to be supportive, at least in the short term. When this happens, seeking support from friends, support groups, and counselors is the best way to ensure everyone's needs are met.

Grieving children, especially, need the constant support of reliable adults. So if your family's grief is causing grown-ups to be inadequately available to any children in their care, ask other grown-ups outside the family for help. Family friends, neighbors, teachers, coaches—many compassionate people will be more than happy to form a network of support if you just ask.

YOUR SIX NEEDS OF MOURNING

"You will lose someone you can't live without, and your heart will be badly broken, and the bad news is that you never completely get over the loss of your beloved. But this is also the good news. They live forever in your broken heart that doesn't seal back up. And you come through. It's like having a broken leg that never heals perfectly—that still hurts when the weather gets cold, but you learn to dance with the limp."

— Anne Lamott

Grief is everything you think and feel inside of you about the death. **Mourning** is expressing those thoughts and feelings outside of yourself. You can think of it as putting your grief into action. Mourning is the work of grief. Mourning is how you come through. Mourning is how you heal.

While every person's grief journey is unique, all grievers share six needs of mourning. These are the actions and activities you must work on in order to process your grief and move toward healing.

Before we review the six needs of mourning, though, I want

to emphasize that mourning can only be done intermittently, in doses. It's often exhausting work. In between times of active mourning, you must rest and replenish your energy. In fact, if you focus on nothing but your loss and grief too much, you will likely become stuck in your journey to healing. So be sure to balance time spent on mourning with time spent on more neutral or enjoyable activities. Build time for respite and distraction into every day as well.

1. ACKNOWLEDGE THE REALITY OF THE DEATH

You must gently confront the difficult reality that someone you love has died and will never be physically present to you again. In cases of sudden and unexpected death, which includes most overdose deaths, this need can be especially challenging. Acknowledging the full reality of the loss may take weeks, months, and sometimes even years.

At times you may push away the reality of the death. This is normal. You will come to integrate the reality in doses as you are ready. It takes time to become accustomed to thinking and feeling in your new reality. Go slowly. There are no rewards for speed.

Ways to work on, or actively mourn, the reality of the death include talking to others about what happened, writing about it in a journal, and spending time looking at photos and memorabilia of the person who died. All of these activities will help you, little by little, move deeper and deeper into acknowledging the reality of the death.

If you have been avoiding learning more about the person's drug use or overdose incident itself, it's important to consider filling in the gaps in your knowledge. Ironically, the more you understand about what happened, the less powerful it becomes. Your fears and imaginings are likely more terrible than the reality. Coming to terms with the facts and details are part of your journey to acceptance and healing.

Especially in cases of traumatic death, acknowledging the reality of what happened is the linchpin need of mourning. If you get stuck in ongoing avoidance or denial in any way, this will inhibit your ability to meet all five of the remaining mourning needs. Gently, bit by bit, and with the support of others, step toward becoming fully acquainted with and accepting the reality so that you can eventually live with purpose and meaning again.

2. EMBRACE THE PAIN OF THE LOSS

To heal in grief, it's necessary to befriend grief. This seems counterintuitive to many people, but it's true. Grief is not something to be ignored or avoided. Instead, it's something to be attended to and embraced, because it is part and parcel of love.

Whenever you are feeling the pain of the loss, I encourage you to stop for a moment and pay attention to the pain. Acknowledge its presence. Affirm its normalcy. Honor its connection to the love and other feelings you still have for the person who died.

As with acknowledging the reality of the loss, ways to mourn the pain you feel inside include talking to good listeners about how you are feeling and what you are thinking, writing down your thoughts and feelings, and allowing yourself to cry or yell or wail whenever your grief needs a relief valve.

When pain is resisted, it intensifies. You don't want to fight with your pain; you want to acknowledge and express it in doses so that eventually you can move from darkness into light.

3. REMEMBER THE PERSON WHO DIED

When someone loved dies, they live on in us through memory. No doubt you have been thinking about the person who died. You may be replaying memories in your head. You might be imagining the overdose incident. It is more common for grievers to ruminate on bad memories in the beginning. If this is true for you, trust that over time and with the work of mourning, you will be able to recall better memories more and more.

To heal, you need to actively remember the person who died

and honor the life that was lived—both the good and the bad. It will help you and others to talk about the person who died and what happened at the time of the overdose. It will help you to display photos of the person who died. It will help you to look through photo albums, read old letters or texts, and watch videos of the person who died.

Yes, remembering someone who has died is often painful, especially in the beginning. This is especially true of overdose deaths, because so many difficult thoughts and feelings are probably competing with your loving, fond memories of this person. But remembering the past makes hoping for the future possible.

4. DEVELOP A NEW SELF-IDENTITY

Part of your self-identity was formed by your relationship with the person who died, which has now changed. For example, you may have gone from being a parent to a bereaved parent or a wife to a widow. The way you thought of yourself and the ways others think of you have been altered.

The overdose complicates this normal and necessary need of mourning. You are now someone whose life has been forever changed by an overdose death. You are part of a community of millions of overdose grievers that you never wanted to be a part of. This can feel like being a member of a club that you hoped and prayed you would never have to join.

Essentially, drug abuse and the premature death of a loved one have become significant threads in your life story. Weaving these unwanted additions into the fabric of your life is arduous and painful work. Who are you now? How will your self and your life be different from now on? Working on answers to these questions is part of this mourning need.

Remember that it's necessary to not only feel and think about this need inside of yourself (to grieve it) but also to express it outside of yourself (to mourn it). Talking to nonjudgmental listeners about what's on your mind and heart is always, always a good idea. This need can also be expressed through journaling, creating artwork, participating in mindfulness practices, and trying out different roles and directions in your life.

For this mourning need, especially, you'll find it helpful to share with other people who have suffered the drug-overdose death of a loved one. Whether in-person or online, support groups for this type of loss are an excellent option. Organizations that serve drug-overdose grievers, like Grief Recovery After Passing, or GRASP, have founded local chapters across the country and also run online support forums on social platforms such as Facebook.

5. SEARCH FOR MEANING

When someone loved dies suddenly and senselessly, it's natural to question the meaning of life and death. "Why?" questions may surface uncontrollably and often precede "How?" questions. "Why did this happen?" often comes before "How will I go on living?"

You will probably question your philosophy of life and explore religious and spiritual beliefs and values as you work on this need. Remember that having faith or spirituality does not negate your need to mourn. It's OK to be sad or in despair even if you believe in an afterlife, for example. It's normal to be angry at God or a higher power. It's natural to feel, for a while, that life has no meaning or is unfair, not worth it, or hopeless.

At its core, grief is a spiritual journey. Working on spiritual questions and needs is absolutely essential to healing. As you grieve, be sure to make time for spirituality, whatever this means for you. You may want to attend a place of worship or regularly visit a spiritual location. You may turn to daily prayer and/or meditation. You might reach out to spiritual or religious leaders or mentors for counseling or informal discussions.

Keep in mind that searching for meaning is a normal part of the grief journey, even if you never feel that you find definitive answers. It's the search that's important at first, and eventually the achievement of a sense of peace with the mystery of life and death.

6. RECEIVE ONGOING SUPPORT FROM OTHERS

As mourners, we need the love and understanding of others if we are to heal. Unfortunately, because of the stigma associated with overdose death, you might find it challenging to get this mourning need met.

Try not to take it personally if others avoid, rebuff, or even blame you for what happened—although I know this is hard and unfair. They usually lack education and awareness. Even in your pain, you can reach out to and educate others. You can let them know what you are feeling. You can talk openly about the circumstances of the death as well as your grief. And you can also choose empathy whenever possible.

Others who have suffered an overdose death can often be the best helpers with this mourning need. They understand and can provide you with the balm of affirmation and empathy. Try to find a drug-overdose survivor support group in your area. Professional counseling is another excellent idea. Because overdose-death grief is naturally complicated, an experienced, compassionate grief counselor can be indispensable in helping you through your most challenging weeks and months.

Outside of this group, look for the listeners. I typically find that about a third of the people in your life will be neutral when it comes to grief support, while another third will be toxic. Avoid this second group at all costs. But the remaining third of people are usually true helpers. They are able to listen without judgment or advice-giving. They understand that what you need is their reliable presence. Turn to this final third anytime you need compassionate support.

Whenever you are feeling your grief, I want you to think about the six needs of mourning. Taking action by expressing your grief outside of yourself in one or more of these six ways will give momentum to your healing. Get in the habit of thinking to yourself: "I am feeling my grief right now. So what can I *do* with it right now?"

Once you have made it through the early days, I encourage you to not be just a passive experiencer of your grief. Instead, be a doer. Active, outward-directed participation in your grief will help you begin to reconcile your loss and find hope and meaning again.

PRIORITIZING GOOD BASIC SELF-CARE

"I now see how owning our story and loving ourselves through that process is the bravest thing we will ever do."

— Brené Brown

If there was ever a time to be dedicated to good basic self-care, it's now. Remember how I said you should think of yourself as being in need of emotional intensive care? The same goes for basic physical, cognitive, social, and spiritual care. When you are grieving, all of these aspects of your self need your compassionate time and attention every single day.

PHYSICAL SELF-CARE

First, grief is naturally fatiguing, so I encourage you to lay your body down two or three times a day for 20 minutes, just to rest. And if you're not sleeping well, see your primary-care physician to talk about your sleep issues. Insomnia negatively affects everything, so it's essential to find solutions to any sleep problems. You won't be able to grieve and mourn effectively if you're not sleeping.

Exercise and eating well are also so important right now. I understand that you might well be struggling to muster the energy or desire to take care of your body these days, but like sleep, these are foundational habits upon which your path to healing will be built. A gentle, slow 20-minute walk each day is a good exercise goal for almost everyone. You don't need to go to a gym or "get in shape"—although if you feel inspired by these activities, by all means, do them. Plus, physical activity can help you mourn your grief. A hike or bike ride is a way to move your body and release your feelings at the same time.

Likewise, feed your body with nutritious foods. In grief, it's easy to fall back on the comfort of bad eating habits, but too much junk food will only compound any grief-related lethargy and depression. Drink lots of water, too, because dehydration adds to fatigue and can also cause headaches, dizziness, and other unpleasant symptoms.

Finally, be aware of any physical compulsions that you might find yourself turning to in an effort to comfort yourself in grief. Self-treating your grief with alcohol or drugs may be tempting, but keep in mind that it's easy for occasional use to turn into abuse. When it comes to finding the momentum to move toward renewed meaning in life, you'll find more success if you remain clean and sober.

COGNITIVE SELF-CARE

Disorganized, chaotic thinking is a common symptom in grief.
You might find yourself unable to concentrate or complete
simple tasks. You might forget simple information.

You're not losing your mind! What's happening is that right
now part of your brain is always thinking about the death
and its consequences. The death—especially the sudden,
unexpected death—of someone who was a big part of your
life and very much alive not long ago is a challenging concept
for the human mind to accept, so it keeps returning to it. Over
time, as your brain learns to adjust to the new reality, trust that
your thinking skills will return.

In the meantime, care for your mind by not overtaxing it.
Take some time off work if you can, and offload any tasks
that are overly challenging. Set aside optional projects. Don't
take on new projects. Give your brain lots of opportunities to
take it easy.

But do consider trying diversions that may soothe your mind.
Meditation, for example, is a great cognitive-stress reliever, as
are yoga and really any physical activity you find enjoyable.
You might find other tactile, "mindless" activities calming to
your mind as well, such as knitting, gardening, video-gaming,
or making artwork.

EMOTIONAL SELF-CARE

We focused on emotional self-care in the "Your Six Needs of Mourning" section (pg. 19). But here I would just like to reiterate that you need and deserve all of the emotional tender loving care you can get right now.

Learn to pay close attention to your emotions. Check in with yourself several times a day and ask, "How am I feeling right now?" Name the feeling(s), and then take a moment to honor them and give them expression.

As you're attending to your emotions, it helps many mourners to learn to distinguish between "clean pain" and "dirty pain." What's the difference? Clean pain is the normal pain that follows difficult life experiences. Dirty pain is the damaging, multiplied pain we create when we catastrophize, judge ourselves, or allow ourselves to be judged by others.

When someone we love dies, for example, we naturally experience grief. That is clean pain. But when we become frozen by worry that we did something wrong, or when we assume that others think badly of us (when in fact we don't really know what they think), or when we feel like we "should" be doing something differently than we are and so feel bad about it, we're experiencing dirty pain.

Most of us experience both kinds of pain, but learning to tell the two apart can help us understand the appropriateness of proper sorrows of the soul. If you feel you are struggling with dirty pain, I encourage you to get the additional support that you need and deserve.

A WORD ABOUT TRIGGERS AND GRIEFBURSTS

As you move forward in your grief journey and eventually begin to heal, you will still experience powerful feelings of loss triggered by a sight, a sound (such as a certain piece of music), a smell, or a memory. You might glimpse someone who looks like the person who died. Or you might see others enjoying life's milestones—such as a graduation, wedding, or birth of a grandchild—and feel a stab of pain knowing your loved one (and by extension, you) will never have these experiences.

It's normal for your grief to be triggered like this, even long into the future. I call these often-unexpected moments of intense grief "griefbursts." They can be so painful they can take your breath away or bring you to your knees.

But I don't recommend withdrawing from the world to avoid life's celebrations, either. Instead, make a plan for what you will do when you experience your next griefburst. You might want to temporarily retreat to your car or another private place and have a good cry. Or you might want to call a close friend or spend a few minutes writing in a journal. Expressing these intense feelings for even just a few minutes usually softens them. In fact, you'll find that if you befriend your griefbursts, they'll have less power over you and your ability to continue to live a life of connection and meaning.

SOCIAL SELF-CARE

People are social creatures, even when—and sometimes *especially* when!—they're grieving.

As I've already emphasized several times, you need the loving support of other people during your time of grief. You need them so you can mourn your grief, i.e., express your grief outside yourself. You need them to listen and to empathize.

But you also need other people because loving, caring relationships are what make life worth living. You have lost one love of your life, and you know all too well how hard that is. But you also may be coming to realize that love is always worth it. In other words, to paraphrase the famous quote by Alfred Lord Tennyson, it's better to have loved and lost than to have never loved at all.

Likewise, fostering relationships and social connection in grief can be challenging in lots of ways, but it's worth it. I'm not saying you must be a social butterfly right now. Nor am I saying you should be hanging around with people who make you feel bad. No. What you do need, though, is to participate in select social and relationship activities that help you feel loved by others and engaged with life.

Good social self-care in grief entails plugging into at least some social activities and family gatherings with people you enjoy and who care about you. Don't over-commit, but also don't over-isolate. Loving relationships are key to helping you find renewed hope and meaning in life again.

SPIRITUAL SELF-CARE

You might think of yourself as a religious or spiritual person, or you might not. But even if you don't consider yourself religious or spiritual, this section applies to you as well.

We talked about the need for spiritual self-care under mourning need 5: search for meaning (pg. 25). Because grief is largely a spiritual journey, spiritual self-care could not be more essential.

What I mean by spiritual self-care is to set aside some time—every day, if you can—to focus on rebuilding and restoring meaning in your life. What gives you a sense of purpose? What gives you a feeling of satisfaction? What gives you joy? When you come to the end of your life, which relationships and activities will stand out as the most meaningful? Whatever the answers to these questions are for you, they're where your spirit lives. Spending at least a few minutes each day in service of these highest-level pursuits is what spiritual self-care is all about.

Right now, in grief, you may be struggling to find answers to these questions. You may have thought you knew the answers before the death, but now you're not so sure, or now you've changed your mind. This is normal. The core beliefs of your life have been shaken. So you'll naturally be working on reconstructing old beliefs or creating entirely new ones.

So whatever feeds your spirit—do that. It might simply be walking or hiking in nature. It might be volunteering. Maybe it's spending time with your family or grandchildren (or pets!). Maybe it's attending services at a church or another place of worship, or taking part in other rituals. Maybe it's meditating or working on mindfulness. Creating art, engaging in physical play/sports, gardening, cooking—these activities and many others might be among those that feed your spirit.

As with all the other aspects of good self-care we've been reviewing in this section, spiritual self-care is not a quick fix for grief. But it is a catalyst. The regular, deliberate feeding of your spirit will help you move through the darkest days of your grief more effectively and find new meaning and purpose again more readily.

Nothing will take away your grief because, we hope, nothing will take away your love. But excellent self-care in these five realms will help you feel better even as you grieve. It will help you continue to live and love as well as possible even on the most difficult of days.

10 THINGS YOU CAN DO WITH YOUR GRIEF TODAY

When you feel stuck in your grief or need some immediate relief, take a look at this list. Pick something to do right here, right now, that will not only help you through the day but will also give you some momentum toward longer-term healing.

1. **Write a thank-you note**
   Drop a note to someone who helped care for the person who died, such as a counselor, paramedic, or friend.

2. **Call a friend**
   Call someone you care about but haven't spoken to in a while. Tell them about the death and how you are doing.

3. **Go for a nature walk**
   Pick a beautiful outdoor setting and go for a walk. Focus on appreciating your surroundings. Or just sit in the sun and let it shine on your face and into your heart.

4. **Cook something you enjoy**
   Studies show that cooking and baking ease depression.

5. **Turn on some music**
   Play your favorite tunes, or choose selections that remind you of happy times with the person who died.

6. **Make a memory box**
   Gather up photos and special objects that remind you of the person who died and put them in a special container. Display this container in a place you will see it frequently.

7. **Look into volunteering**
   When we're ready, helping others helps us heal. Volunteer for an organization or cause that's meaningful to you.

8. **Pray or meditate**

   Both practices can calm the mind and unburden the heart.

9. **Visit the cemetery or final resting place**

   Being near the remains of the person who died may help you embrace both your love and your grief.

10. **Do something you've always wanted to do**

    Grief has a way of shaking things up. Make use of this opportunity by taking action on something you've been putting off for a long time.

RECONCILING YOUR GRIEF

"My scars are a testament to the love and the relationship
that I had for and with the person who died.
And if the scar is deep, so was the love."
— **Author unknown**

Over time, if you actively work to meet your six needs of mourning and take good care of yourself in all five of the realms we discussed, your grief will naturally begin to soften. It will not end. It will not "go away." You will not "get over it." Instead, your grief will become integrated into your life. Like everything else that has ever happened to you, it will become part of who you are.

I call this phase of grief "reconciliation." You'll know that you're moving toward reconciliation when the death is no longer the first thing you think about each day. Other signs of reconciliation include:

- a return to stable eating and sleeping patterns

- the capacity to enjoy experiences in life that you normally find enjoyable

- the ability to live a full life without feelings of guilt or shame

- the drive to organize and plan your life toward the future

- the adaptability to accommodate more change into your life

- the acquaintance of new parts of yourself that you have discovered during your grief journey

- the serenity to be comfortable with the way things are rather than attempting to make them as they were

- the awareness that you do not "get over" your grief but instead build a new reality, meaning, and purpose

- the acknowledgment that the pain of loss is inextricable from the joy of love

- the embracing of the transformed you

Reconciliation emerges the way grass grows. You may not notice your grass growing each day, but soon you come to realize it's time to cut the grass again. Likewise, you can't see from one day to the next that you are healing in grief, but eventually, over the course of months and years, you will grow aware that you have come a long way.

In grief, healing means to become whole again. Your loss has torn you apart, and in reconciliation you will find yourself put back together. No, you will not be the same as you were before the death. Instead, the injury will be a fully integrated part of you. Trust that you can and will reach reconciliation if you keep actively expressing your grief through the six needs of mourning.

In reconciliation, some people who have suffered the overdose death of a loved one eventually find ways to live their lives with deeper meaning and purpose. Many go on to help others struggling with addiction or loss. Others become advocates for change. And some simply begin to live each day with a new appreciation for the now.

FINDING HOPE AGAIN

"Life has ripped a great big chunk out of me.
But I'm patching the hole."
— Author unknown

If you're feeling hopeless right now, I want you to know that I hear you, and I understand. You have every right to feel sad, angry, lonely, and yes, hopeless.

Feeling hopeless is understandable in the aftermath of a drug-overdose death. Your world has been torn apart. Your present is full of pain, and your hopes and dreams for the future may feel shattered.

Yet still, you have the power within you to rebuild hope. Life is full of heartbreak, but it is also full of joy, love, and meaning.

As I've mentioned, hope is an expectation of a good that is yet to be. If you believe that your future can include moments of joy, love, and meaning, you have within you a spark of hope. And now part of your essential grief work is to nurture that spark.

How do you nurture the spark of hope?

- You nurture hope by spending time with the people and pets you love.

- You nurture hope by taking part in activities you care about.

- You nurture hope by engaging in spiritual practices.

- You nurture hope by making future plans that you will enjoy.

- You nurture hope by helping others.

- You nurture hope by taking care of your body, your mind, your heart, your social connections, and your soul.

The more you nurture your spark of hope, the more it will grow. The spark will become a flame, and the flame can become a fire. And even on days when the fire ebbs and fades to embers temporarily, you'll know that you have the power to rebuild it again in all of the ways listed above.

A FINAL WORD

"Death is a challenge. It tells us not to waste time."
— Author unknown

Your grief journey has been complicated by an unexpected, untimely, and stigmatized death. It will not be easy.

Grieving this death will likely be harder than other deaths you have experienced, which makes the mourning harder too. I sometimes refer to the mourning required of traumatic losses as "heroic mourning." The idea is this: If this grief feels bigger and more painful than other griefs you have suffered in your life, it will demand bigger and bolder expression, too.

So I wish you both courage and hope on this journey. And I know that if you boldly commit to meeting your six needs of mourning, now and for as long as you need to, you will find your way to reconciliation and continued meaning in life and living.

Right now, I invite you to close your eyes and remember the person who died. Picture them at their happiest and healthiest. Recall their special smile. Feel your love for them. That will never die.

THE OVERDOSE-DEATH MOURNER'S BILL OF RIGHTS

Though you should reach out to others as you do the work of mourning, you should not feel obligated to accept the unhelpful responses you may receive from some people. You are the one who is grieving, and as such, you have certain "rights" no one should try to take away from you.

1. *You have the right to experience your own unique grief.*
   No one else will grieve this death in exactly the same way you do. So, when you turn to others for help, don't allow them to tell what you should or should not be feeling. And try not to judge others for how they are grieving, either.

2. *You have the right to talk about your grief.*
   Talking about your grief as well as the circumstances of the overdose will help you heal. Seek out others who will allow you to talk as much as you want, as often as you want, about your grief. If at times you don't feel like talking, you also have the right to be silent—just don't remain silent for too long.

3. *You have the right to feel a multitude of emotions.*
   Shock, anger, fear, guilt, and relief are just a few of the
   emotions you might experience as part of your grief
   journey. None of your feelings are wrong, but all need to
   be expressed. Find listeners who will accept your feelings
   without condition.

4. *You have the right to fight back against any shame and stigma.*
   The stigma associated with addiction and drug-overdose
   deaths is wrong. You have the right to reject shame and
   stand for openness, honesty, and love.

5. *You have the right to be tolerant of your physical and emotional
   limits.* Your feelings of loss and sadness will probably leave
   you feeling fatigued. Respect what your body and mind are
   telling you. Get daily rest. Eat balanced meals. And don't
   allow others to push you into doing things you don't feel
   ready to do.

6. *You have the right to experience "griefbursts."*
   Sometimes, out of nowhere, a powerful surge of grief may
   overcome you. This can be frightening, but it is normal and
   natural. Find someone who understands and will let you
   talk it out.

7. *You have the right to embrace your spirituality.*
   If faith or spirituality is a part of your life, express it in ways
   that feel right to you. Allow yourself to be around people

who understand and support your religious or spiritual beliefs.

8. *You have the right to search for meaning.*
   You may find yourself asking, "Why did he or she die? Why this way? Why now?" Some of your questions may have answers, but some may not. And watch out for the clichéd responses some people may give you. Comments like "It was God's will" or "Keep real busy" are not helpful, and you do not have to accept them.

9. *You have the right to treasure good memories.*
   Happy memories are one of the best legacies that exist after the death of someone loved. You will always remember. Instead of ignoring your memories, find others with whom you can share them.

10. *You have the right to move toward your grief and heal.*
    Reconciling your grief, which has been complicated by the circumstances of the drug use and overdose, will not happen quickly. Be patient and tolerant with yourself, and avoid people who are impatient and intolerant with you. Neither you nor those around you must forget that the death of the person you loved will change your life forever.

RESOURCES

Center on Addiction
centeronaddiction.org

The Courage to Speak Foundation
couragetospeak.org

GRASP: Grief Recovery After a Substance Passing
grasphelp.org

International Overdose Awareness Day
overdoseday.com

Narcotics Overdose Prevention & Educational Task Force
nopetaskforce.org

Survivor Resources
survivorresources.org

Verywell Mind
verywellmind.com

ALSO BY ALAN WOLFELT

The Journey Through Grief
REFLECTIONS ON HEALING

SECOND EDITION

This revised, second edition of *The Journey Through Grief* takes Dr. Wolfelt's popular book of reflections and adds space for guided journaling, asking readers thoughtful questions about their unique mourning needs and providing room to write responses.

The Journey Through Grief is organized around the six needs that all mourners must yield to—indeed embrace—if they are to go on to find continued meaning in life and living. Following a short explanation of each mourning need is a series of brief, spiritual passages that, when read slowly and reflectively, help mourners work through their unique thoughts and feelings.

ISBN 978-1-879651-11-1 • 152 pages • hardcover • $21.95

All Dr. Wolfelt's publications can be ordered by mail from:
Companion Press, 3735 Broken Bow Road, Fort Collins, CO 80526
(970) 226-6050 • www.centerforloss.com

ALSO BY ALAN WOLFELT

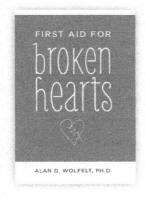

First Aid for Broken Hearts

Life is both wonderful and devastating. It graces us with joy, and it breaks our hearts. If your heart is broken, this book is for you.

Whether you're struggling with a death, break-up, illness, unwanted life change, or loss of any kind, this book will help you both understand your predicament and figure out what to do about it.

Loss may be an unavoidable part of human life, but it doesn't have to prevent you from living well. You can and will survive this. Actually, if you adopt this guide's basic principles, revealed and tested by one of the world's most beloved grief counselors, you will even go on to thrive. Let's get mending.

ISBN: 978-1-61722-281-8 • softcover • $9.95

All Dr. Wolfelt's publications can be ordered by mail from:
Companion Press, 3735 Broken Bow Road, Fort Collins, CO 80526
(970) 226-6050 • www.centerforloss.com

ALSO BY ALAN WOLFELT

The Wilderness of Grief

A BEAUTIFUL, HARDCOVER GIFT BOOK
VERSION OF *UNDERSTANDING YOUR GRIEF*

The Wilderness of Grief is an excerpted version of *Understanding Your Grief*, making it approachable and appropriate for all mourners.

This concise book makes an excellent gift for anyone in mourning. On the book's inside front cover is room for writing an inscription to your grieving friend.

While some readers will appreciate the more in-depth *Understanding Your Grief*, others may feel overwhelmed by the amount of information it contains. For these readers we recommend *The Wilderness of Grief*. (Fans of *Understanding Your Grief* will also want a copy of *The Wilderness of Grief* to turn to in spare moments.)

This is an ideal book for the bedside or coffee table. Pick it up before bed and read just a few pages. You'll be carried off to sleep by its gentle, affirming messages of hope and healing.

ISBN 978-1-879651-52-4 • 112 pages • hardcover • $15.95

All Dr. Wolfelt's publications can be ordered by mail from:
Companion Press, 3735 Broken Bow Road, Fort Collins, CO 80526
(970) 226-6050 • www.centerforloss.com

ALSO BY ALAN WOLFELT

Grief One Day at a Time

365 MEDITATIONS TO HELP YOU
HEAL AFTER LOSS

After someone you love dies, each day can be a struggle. But each day, you can also find comfort and understanding in this daily companion. With one brief entry for every day of the calendar year, this little book offers small, one-day-at-a-time doses of guidance and healing. Each entry includes an inspiring or soothing quote followed by a short discussion of the day's theme.

How do you get through the loss of a loved one? One day at a time. This compassionate gem of a book will accompany you.

ISBN 978-1-61722-238-2 • 384 pages • softcover • $14.95

All Dr. Wolfelt's publications can be ordered by mail from:
Companion Press, 3735 Broken Bow Road, Fort Collins, CO 80526
(970) 226-6050 • www.centerforloss.com